MEETING *the* SPIRIT

10 studies
for individuals or groups

Douglas Connelly

With Notes for Leaders

Scripture Union is an international Christian charity working with churches in more than 130 countries.

Thank you for purchasing this book. Any profits from this book support SU in England and Wales to bring the good news of Jesus Christ to children, young people and families and to enable them to meet God through the Bible and prayer.

Find out more about our work and how you can get involved at:

www.scriptureunion.org.uk (England and Wales)
www.suscotland.org.uk (Scotland)
www.suni.co.uk (Northern Ireland)
www.scriptureunion.org (USA)
www.su.org.au (Australia)

ISBN 978 1 85999 799 4

First published in the United States by InterVarsity Press 1993, revised 2003.
© Douglas Connelly

This edition published in the United Kingdom © Scripture Union 2000, reprinted 2005, 2007, 2009, 2012, 2015, 2016.

Scripture quotations, unless otherwise indicated, are taken from the Holy Bible, New International Version. Copyright © 1973, 1978, 1984 by International Bible Society. Anglicisation copyright © 1979, 1984, 1989. Used by permission of Hodder and Stoughton Limited.

British Library Cataloguing-in-Publication data: a catalogue record for this book is available from the British Library.

Printed in India by Thomson Press India Ltd.

Contents

Getting the Most Out of
Meeting the Spirit

I'm afraid that many followers of Jesus Christ know about as much concerning the Holy Spirit as certain disciples who were asked by the apostle Paul, "Did you receive the Holy Spirit when you believed?" They responded, "No, we have not even heard that there is a Holy Spirit!"

Those particular disciples were followers of John the Baptist, and I'm sure they had heard John preach about the Holy Spirit. What they had not yet realized, however, was that the Holy Spirit promised by God was available to them. They had never heard that the Holy Spirit could make a difference in their lives. Christians today have certainly heard about the Holy Spirit, but many of us have never encountered the Spirit in a life-changing way.

That is what this study guide is intended to do in your life—change it! We will examine key passages of Scripture that teach us vital truths about who the Spirit of God is and what he is anxious to do in our lives. But the goal is not simply to gain more knowledge. Our goal is to translate that knowledge into a deeper relationship with another person—a divine person, the Spirit of God. You are embarking on an exciting journey—but be prepared to be changed!

Three basic biblical facts will underlie everything we discuss together about the Spirit of God. The first fact is that the Spirit *is*. He exists. Belief in the Holy Spirit is not based on myth or on a religious fairy tale. As we will see, Jesus referred to the Spirit repeatedly. Every New Testament writer and many Old Testament writers talk about the Spirit of God.

The second basic fact about the Spirit is that he is a person. Christians (following the biblical example) refer to the Spirit as "he," not as "it." *Spirit* is not simply a term for God's energy or God's movement in our hearts. The Spirit is a personal being. Because he is a person, we can relate to the Spirit in a personal way. In fact, he wants us to know him on a deeply intimate level.

The Bible is also clear in its declaration that the Spirit is a divine person. He is God. Since the first century, Christians have consistently recognized the Spirit as a member of the Trinity—God the Father, God the Son, and God the Holy Spirit. The Spirit's deity will be confirmed repeatedly as we explore the Scripture passages in this study guide.

The fact that the Spirit is God opens up all kinds of wonderful possibilities for us. As we come to develop a personal relationship with the Spirit, we are developing a relationship with God himself. Most of us already relate with Jesus, and we know how to interact with God the Father. Now we will see what it means to walk in the realm of the Spirit.

The Spirit of God already knows us completely. We have the opportunity through these studies to grow in our knowledge of the Spirit.

Suggestions for Individual Study

1. As you begin each study, pray that God will speak to you through his Word.

2. Read the introduction to the study and respond to the personal reflection question or exercise. This is designed to help you focus on God and on the theme of the study.

3. Each study deals with a particular passage—so that you can delve into the author's meaning in that context. Read and reread the passage to be studied. The questions are written using the language of the New International Version, so you may wish to use that version of the Bible. The New Revised Standard Version is also recommended.

4. This is an inductive Bible study, designed to help you discover for yourself what Scripture is saying. The study includes three types of questions. *Observation* questions ask about the basic facts: who, what, when, where and how. *Interpretation* questions delve into the meaning of the passage. *Application* questions help you discover the implications of the text for growing in Christ. These three keys unlock the treasures of Scripture.

Write your answers to the questions in the spaces provided or in a personal journal. Writing can bring clarity and deeper understanding of yourself and of God's Word.

5. It might be good to have a Bible dictionary handy. Use it to look up any unfamiliar words, names or places.

6. Use the prayer suggestion to guide you in thanking God for what you have learned and to pray about the applications that have come to mind.

7. You may want to go on to the suggestion under "Now or Later," or you may want to use that idea for your next study.

Suggestions for Members of a Group Study

1. Come to the study prepared. Follow the suggestions for individual study mentioned above. You will find that careful preparation will greatly enrich your time spent in group discussion.

2. Be willing to participate in the discussion. The leader of your group will not be lecturing. Instead, he or she will be encouraging the members of the group to discuss what they have learned. The leader will be asking the questions that are found in this guide.

3. Stick to the topic being discussed. Your answers should be based on the verses which are the focus of the discussion and not on outside authorities such as commentaries or speakers. These studies focus on a particular passage of Scripture. Only rarely should you refer to other portions of the Bible. This allows for everyone to participate in in-depth study on equal ground.

4. Be sensitive to the other members of the group. Listen attentively when they describe what they have learned. You may be surprised by their insights! Each question assumes a variety of answers. Many questions do not have "right" answers, particularly questions that aim at meaning or application. Instead the questions push us to explore the passage more thoroughly.

When possible, link what you say to the comments of others. Also, be affirming whenever you can. This will encourage some of the more hesitant members of the group to participate.

5. Be careful not to dominate the discussion. We are sometimes so eager to express our thoughts that we leave too little opportunity for others to respond. By all means participate! But allow others to also.

6. Expect God to teach you through the passage being discussed and through the other members of the group. Pray that you will have an enjoyable and profitable time together, but also that as a result of the study you will find ways that you can take action individually and/or as a group.

7. Remember that anything said in the group is considered confidential and should not be discussed outside the group unless specific permission is given to do so.

8. If you are the group leader, you will find additional suggestions at the back of the guide.

1

Meet the
Holy Spirit!

I sometimes find it awkward to meet new people. I don't always know what to say or how to relate. It's always easier to meet someone if we are introduced to each other by a mutual friend. The person who knows us both can help us overcome those difficult initial hurdles. As we think about meeting the Spirit, we can count on Jesus to make the introduction.

GROUP DISCUSSION. What impressions come to your mind when you think about the Holy Spirit?

PERSONAL REFLECTION. What words would you use to describe your relationship with the Holy Spirit—distant or intimate, cautious or close? What fears do you have about coming into a closer relationship with God the Holy Spirit?

John chapters 13—17 contain Jesus' final instructions to his disciples before his death on the cross. He tells them that he is leaving and that they won't be coming with him. *Read John 16:5-15.*

1. Describe the mood of the disciples as Jesus speaks to them.

2. Given the setting, why do you think Jesus refers to the Spirit as "the Counselor"?

3. In what ways is it to the disciples' advantage that Jesus would go away and the Spirit of God would come?

4. In verses 8-11 Jesus outlines the ministry of the Spirit to the world. According to these verses, what specific conviction does the Spirit bring to those who hear the message of Christ?

5. The "prince of this world" mentioned in verse 11 is Satan. Why is it important for the Spirit to convince the world that their "prince" is already condemned?

6. Based on verses 12 and 13, how would you describe the Spirit's ministry to Jesus' followers?

7. The disciples listening to Jesus would later record the message of Christ in the books and letters of the New Testament. What authority does Jesus' statement impart to those writings?

8. What insight can you gain from verses 14 and 15 about the Spirit's relationship to Jesus and to the Father?

9. Of the different ministries of the Holy Spirit described in this passage, which one do you need most in your life right now and why?

10. What are your expectations as you pursue a deeper relationship with the Spirit?

Ask the Holy Spirit to give you an open heart to all that he wants to do in you through this study.

Now or Later
Jesus called the Holy Spirit the Counselor (or the Comforter). When have you experienced comfort or encouragement from God?

How can you draw more on this promised resource?

2

The Spirit Invades

When God is about to do something new, he has a powerful way of announcing it. In the Old Testament God rescued his people from slavery with a mighty outpouring of his power. When Jesus, God's own Son, was condemned and executed, God brought him back to life in an unparalleled act of power. When God was prepared to push a few reluctant disciples along on the path of world evangelization, he swept over them in another work of power. God sent the Holy Spirit.

GROUP DISCUSSION. Have you ever been in a worship service or prayer group and sensed the Spirit moving in a powerful way? Describe that experience and its results in your life.

PERSONAL REFLECTION. When have you sensed God's power at work in your heart? What happened (or, what would you want to happen)?

The Holy Spirit had been present in the world and in the lives of God's people since the beginning. But on the day of Pentecost, something radically changed. The Spirit came in a new way. Believers were thrust out with a new message. A new mission had begun. *Read Acts 2:1-13.*

1. What aspects of verses 1-4 would you want to capture on videotape?

What would a sound track of those verses sound like?

2. What is the reaction of the crowd?

If you had seen this event, how do you think you would have responded?

3. *Read Acts 2:14-41.* What explanation does Peter give for the events that were occurring?

4. Based on Peter's quotation from the Old Testament (from Joel 2:28-32), what would you expect to see and experience when God poured out his Spirit on all people?

5. The crowd already knew about Jesus' ministry, miracles and death. What is new in Peter's message (vv. 22-36)?

6. What does Peter promise to those who repent and believe in Jesus (v. 38)?

7. *Read Acts 2:42-47.* What can you discover in these verses about the activities and attitudes of the early Christians?

8. Which of these elements are missing in your church or Christian fellowship group?

9. How can you be more open to the Holy Spirit to restore some of these basic elements of Christian faith and ministry to your church or small group?

Ask the Holy Spirit to give you the courage to talk with other people about Jesus.

Now or Later

Think back to the last time you talked with a non-Christian about Jesus (or the last time you heard the gospel presented in a church service). Which elements of Peter's sermon were included in the presentation? Which elements were missing?

3

The Spirit Speaks

1 Corinthians 2

The fifth inning of a televised baseball game is a great time for a nap! One recent Sunday afternoon I had drifted blissfully off to sleep when a series of loud beeps from the television brought me fully awake. The beeps were followed by this announcement: "We interrupt this program to bring you a severe weather bulletin." By now I was sitting up, listening intently to the message that followed. My wife, who had been in another room, was standing in the doorway, totally focused on the warning from our regional weather center. The words were intensely practical, and they came into our home with authority.

GROUP DISCUSSION. What does it take for someone to get your attention—the silent treatment? verbal confrontation? crying? How do you respond when you know someone is trying to communicate with you?

PERSONAL REFLECTION. When have you been in a situation where you wished God would speak directly to you? Why did you feel that way?

The Spirit of God speaks with the highest authority—the authority of God himself. But far too often, we are content to yawn our way through it. This study will help us hear God's message with renewed intensity. *Read 1 Corinthians 2:1-16.*

---

1. Describe the *content* of Paul's message to the Corinthians.

Describe the *spirit* of Paul as God's messenger.

---

2. Paul thought it was important that his message came to the Corinthians in "the Spirit's power." What would have been the result if Paul had preached only with "wise and persuasive words" (vv. 1-5)?

---

3. What is the end result of following purely human wisdom (vv. 6-8)?

What results from following God's wisdom?

4. According to verses 9-10, what methods fail to uncover the good things that God has prepared for us?

If those methods have failed, how *can* we discover these good things from God?

5. Why would Paul's argument in verses 11 and 12 convince you that the Holy Spirit is God?

6. Since Paul and the other apostles are no longer here to speak to us directly, where can we find these "words taught by the Spirit" (v. 13)?

7. What insights can you gain from verse 14 that may explain why a person might reject the message of Christ and the clear teaching of the Bible?

8. According to this passage, what elements are required for us to have "the mind of Christ"?

9. As the result of your study of this passage, how will you listen to God's Word from now on?

10. What specific things can you ask the Holy Spirit to do in your mind and heart whenever you read and study the Bible?

Thank the Holy Spirit for providing an accurate expression of God's truth in the Bible.

Now or Later

Explore different resources to guide you in your reading of the Bible. *The One-Year Bible,* for example, takes you through the entire Bible in one year. You can start anytime. Other guides will take you through the New Testament or the Psalms. Why not read one short biblical book (like Colossians) every day for a week—or read the book of Proverbs, one chapter a day for a month? Begin by asking the Holy Spirit to be your teacher. Listen for his voice as you read. Be willing to obey what the Spirit says.

4

The Spirit Renews

A few years ago I watched the birth of our third child. Our son Kyle emerged into the bright light of a new world. His first gasp drew air into his lungs. His next act was to let out a piercing cry. Everyone in the delivery room smiled. The cry was a sign of life.

GROUP DISCUSSION. What were you first told about where babies come from, and when (if not at first) did you learn the truth?

PERSONAL REFLECTION. What thoughts and feelings do you associate with birth?

Not long after Kyle was born, I witnessed the birth of a young adult woman! The birth did not take place in a hospital; it happened in a home. As she heard the message of Christ, the young woman believed. At that moment she was born into a whole new spiritual realm. The Spirit was intimately involved in that new birth. I explained the message of the gospel. The young woman received it with faith. But the Spirit brought new life. *Read John 3:1-8.*

1. How would you describe Nicodemus to your friends?

2. Summarize his view of who Jesus was (v. 2).

What was positive and what was lacking?

3. How would you explain Nicodemus's initial understanding of being "born again" (v. 4)?

4. Jesus talks about two births—the first a birth of the flesh, the second a birth of the spirit. Describe each birth in your own words.

5. What role does the Holy Spirit play in the new birth?

6. In what ways is the Spirit's work of bringing people to new birth like the blowing of the wind (v. 8)?

7. How can your understanding of the Spirit's work affect how you talk to others about Jesus?

8. Have you experienced the new birth Jesus talks about in this passage? Tell how the Spirit worked in your life to bring you to Christ.

9. There are obvious signs that a person has physical life. What are the signs that a person has the spiritual life Jesus describes in this passage?

10. Which of these signs of new life is most obvious in your life?

Which is least obvious, and what would it take to change that?

Express your praise to the Spirit for opening your heart to believe in Jesus.

Now or Later

Who is a Nicodemus in your life—someone who has expressed an interest in Jesus but who has not yet believed in him? Plan to communicate more about Jesus with that person this week. Ask the members of your group or a Christian friend to pray with you for the right opportunity. When you meet next, let them know how it went.

5

The Spirit
Empowers

Acts 6:1-15; 7:54-60

The small man was almost hidden by the oak pulpit. His voice was soft. When he began to speak, very few in the audience listened with much interest. Within five minutes, however, every eye was riveted on the speaker. Everyone strained to hear his words. The man had spent years languishing in the prison camps of China for one crime—faith in Jesus Christ.

After Harry Lee spoke, I asked him one question: "How did you survive such abuse and pain?" His answer was immediate. "Whatever I needed for each hour and each crisis, the Holy Spirit provided. Never any excess. Never any lack."*

GROUP DISCUSSION. Have you ever felt special power come over you as you faced a physical emergency or an emotional challenge? Describe that experience.

PERSONAL REFLECTION. In what area of your life do you sense a need for power? Invite the Holy Spirit to use this study to infuse you with dynamic power.

When we hear stories like Harry Lee's survival in a prison camp, most of us think: "He may have sensed God's power in his life, but I've never had that experience in mine." The truth is the Holy Spirit is ready and willing to enable us to face any crisis or opportunity in his strength. *Read Acts 6:1-7.*

---

1. Based on the information in these verses, how would it make you feel to be around Stephen?

---

2. The Holy Spirit will empower Stephen to stand against some incredible opposition. What qualities does Stephen cultivate in his life and character to prepare the way for the Spirit's work?

---

3. *Read Acts 6:8-15.* What is the core of the argument between Stephen and the members of the Synagogue of Freedmen?

---

4. How does the Spirit help Stephen stand against this opposition?

5. In what situations might you ask for the Spirit's help or strength?

6. What do we risk when we speak with the Spirit's power (vv. 11-14)?

7. *Read Acts 7:54-60.* The outcome of Stephen's arrest is his execution. In what ways does the Spirit empower Stephen to face such a cruel death?

8. If you had to choose between being Stephen or one of those who stoned him, which would you choose and why?

9. What words accurately describe your spiritual life?

---

10. In what ways (if any) would your life change if you were "full of faith and of the Holy Spirit"?

Ask God the Spirit to prepare you to be used in a powerful way in your workplace, community or church fellowship.

Now or Later

Read some accounts of Christians who have been imprisoned or martyred for their faith. Find out where Christians are persecuted today and begin to pray for them. Ask for the Spirit's power to be obvious in their lives and in their witness.

---

* Harry Lee's story is told in *From the Claws of the Dragon* by Carroll Hunt (Grand Rapids, Mich.: Zondervan, 1988).

6

The Spirit Guides

"If I just knew what God wanted me to do."

Most of us have said or thought those words as we have faced difficult decisions. Probably no aspect of the Christian life is more frustrating than discovering the will of God.

Two factors contribute to our frustration. First, we usually want God to give us *answers* when what he promises to give us is *wisdom*. Second, we are not aware of the Spirit's work of guiding us through times of uncertainty. Because we don't know that the Spirit is willing and anxious to work in such a way, we don't anticipate his ministry in our lives. As a result, we don't sense the Spirit's leading.

GROUP DISCUSSION. When has someone given you wise direction?

PERSONAL REFLECTION. Think back to a time when you needed the Lord's direction in a decision. How did you seek out God's will?

In this passage from the book of Acts, Paul and his companions experience the Spirit's guidance in a powerful way. *Read Acts 16:1-10.*

1. What factors in verses 1-5 demonstrate that Paul was acting in obedience to the Lord?

2. Paul and his companions first experience the negative leading of the Spirit. They are not allowed to enter certain regions or to preach in some areas (vv. 6-7). How do you think the Spirit told Paul not to proceed into those places?

3. Some Christian believe that Paul made a mistake by even trying to enter those regions. They think Paul should have waited for clear direction from God before taking any initiative. Explain why you agree or disagree with that view.

4. Positive direction from the Spirit came by means of a vision to Paul. What was it about the vision and Paul's circumstances that would lead Paul to conclude "God had called us to preach the gospel" in the new region of Macedonia (v. 10)?

5. What principles can you draw from Paul's experience that will help you know when the Spirit is directing you?

6. *Read Acts 16:11-15.* What facts in these verses confirm that Paul's earlier vision and direction were indeed from the Lord?

7. Should we look for confirming evidence of the Spirit's leading in our lives? (For example, can we determine the Spirit's leading simply by results? If a decision brings difficulty or inconvenience with it, does that mean it was not God's will?) Explain your answer.

8. When you are faced with a decision, what steps will you follow as you seek the Spirit's direction?

9. What specific things will you expect to receive from the Spirit as you anticipate his leading?

10. What practical counsel and help can you offer to another believer who is struggling with discerning the will of God?

Tell the Holy Spirit that you want every decision you make to be guided by his wisdom.

Now or Later

Read James 1:5-8. What assurance do those verses give you about how God will guide you in life decisions?

What warnings should you remember?

7

The Spirit Liberates

Romans 8:1-27

We live in a society that claims to be free. In reality, the people in our culture are often enslaved. The cry of men and women today is to be free to do what they want, when they want, where they want—and call it "freedom." The Bible calls that kind of self-centered lifestyle "slavery."

GROUP DISCUSSION. At what time in your life did you feel most liberated to pursue your dreams?

PERSONAL REFLECTION. What personal freedom would be hardest for you to give up and why?

The source of real liberation is the Spirit of God. He liberates the human spirit from bondage to the old masters of sin and death. We can now serve our new Master with joyful obedience. In Romans 8 the apostle Paul reaches the height of adoration and praise to the life-giving and liberating Spirit. *Read Romans 8:1-27.*

1. How would you describe life for Paul when he lived under the old taskmasters of the law, sin and death?

2. How did God set us free from the condemnation of the law (v. 3)?

3. How does God set us free from being dominated by our sinful nature (vv. 4-9)?

4. How does God set us free from the destruction of death (vv. 10-11)?

5. If we are no longer under obligation to these old masters, why do we choose so often to submit again to their authority?

How can we be more effective in resisting them?

6. One aspect of the Spirit's ministry is to give us confidence before the Father. In what ways does the truth explained in verses 15-17 help you to relate more positively to the Father?

7. Even those of us who have the Spirit of God find ourselves "groaning inwardly" at times as we wait for our full redemption. Is that true in your experience? Explain your answer with specific examples.

8. What promises in verses 18-25 help you face times of difficulty or pain with greater joy and confidence?

9. In what ways does the Spirit minister to us in our weakness (vv. 26-27)?

10. Which of the Spirit's ministries described in this chapter encourages you most at this point in your life?

How will you live differently as a result of your knowledge of that ministry of the Spirit of God to you?

Willingly give yourself and your desires to the Holy Spirit. Ask him to help you live as God's child.

Now or Later

One of the most comforting ministries of the Spirit is that he intercedes for us with God the Father when we don't know what to pray for. *Read Hebrews 7:25.* How does it make you feel to know that Jesus prays for you too?

8

The Spirit Equips

1 Corinthians 12

When I talked to Bill about being part of our church's ushering team, his response was "That's not my gift." Since he had responded the same way to several other positions in ministry, I said, "What exactly is your gift?"

"I'm not sure," he shot back. "I think it's just to be an observer."

I knew from Bill's answer that he wasn't concerned about using "his gift" at all. He simply didn't want any responsibility.

GROUP DISCUSSION. Describe a Christian you know who has a special "gift" and who uses that gift for the Lord.

PERSONAL REFLECTION. What are your areas of giftedness or strength? How have you used that ability recently to bless someone else?

The subject of spiritual gifts has created tremendous debate among Christians. In some circles an emphasis on gifts is all you will hear. In other fellowships the subject is totally avoided. The New Testament, however, presents a very balanced perspective.

Spiritual gifts are not all there is to the Christian life. But the Christian life cannot be lived effectively without using these marvelous grace gifts from God's Spirit. *Read 1 Corinthians 12.*

1. What does the passage tell you about how gifts and the Spirit work together?

2. What does it tell you about how gifts and the body work together?

3. Paul lists several spiritual gifts in verses 8-10. Briefly describe each one and (if you can) give an example of how you have seen that gift demonstrated.

4. Why is it important for Paul to talk about the unity of Christ's body at the same time that he talks about spiritual gifts (vv. 12-20)?

5. In your opinion are spiritual gifts different from natural abilities? Explain your answer.

6. The Spirit links believers in Christ together. In what practical ways should this truth affect the composition of your church or fellowship group?

How should it affect the way you relate to each person in it?

7. Why does Paul emphasize that it is God who has placed the members of the body together as he desires?

8. According to this passage, what specific responsibilities do you have toward other members of the body?

9. What would you say that your spiritual gift or gifts are?

10. How are you using your gifts to build up Christ's body?

Thank the Holy Spirit for giving you spiritual gifts. Express your willing-ness to use your gifts to strengthen and bless other Christians.

Now or Later

You may want to use one of the spiritual gift discovery tests to find areas where your gifts may lie. You can find the tests in Christian bookstores or at various places on the Internet. One of the best ways to discover what your gifts are (or are not) is to volunteer for jobs in your local church and let the Spirit guide you toward your areas of giftedness. Talk with your pastor or a spiritual mentor about minis-tries you can explore.

9

The Spirit Transforms

The television evangelist was captivating in his delivery. The crowd of people seated before him hung on every word. He quoted from the Bible with ease. What made me turn off the program was not his message or his style. It was his arrogance.

GROUP DISCUSSION. How does it affect you when someone approaches you with an unloving or negative spirit?

PERSONAL REFLECTION. Think of Christians you know who display a loving, gracious attitude. In what ways are you like them? In what ways is your attitude not like theirs?

Some Christians are highly gifted and use their gifts to touch a wide audience. As they focus on their gifts, however, they can easily forget the fruit of the Spirit. The presence of the Holy Spirit in our lives does not display itself in what we do as much as in who we are. The evidence of the Spirit's presence is a changed character. *Read Galatians 5:13-26.*

1. As Christians, we have been set free in Christ. According to these verses, what are some of the limitations on that freedom?

2. When do you personally sense the struggle between your sinful nature and the Spirit most strongly?

3. Which of the expressions of the sinful nature outlined in verses 19-21 do you find most apparent in our society?

In what ways is it displayed?

4. What do you think Paul means when he says in verse 21, "Those who live like this will not inherit the kingdom of God"?

5. Why does Paul refer to the qualities in verses 22-26 as the "fruit" of the Spirit?

6. Describe each aspect of the fruit of the Spirit and explain how that quality is demonstrated in a person's life.

7. If we have crucified the sinful nature with its passions and desires as verse 24 says, why then do we struggle with its power?

8. In the context of the passage, what does it mean to "keep in step with the Spirit" (v. 25)?

---

9. As you look over the list of qualities that demonstrate the Spirit's presence in a person's life, which of them is most lacking in your life?

What specific steps can you take to cultivate that quality?

Promise the Holy Spirit that you will strive to "keep in step" with him by living in submission to his will and direction.

Now or Later

Ask someone you love and trust to answer question 9 about you. Be willing to listen to that person's evaluation of your character without becoming defensive or angry. Ask that person to help you strengthen areas of your character that are weak.

10

The Spirit Influences

None of us wants to be controlled by someone else. Particularly in the realm of our spiritual life, we cringe at the thought of someone being in control of our lives. Even the word *control* makes us think of the mindless obedience demanded by certain cults. Their members seem to give up their wills, and even rational thought, in false reverence for a human leader.

GROUP DISCUSSION. Have you ever had another Christian try to dictate how you should live? What was (or would be) your response to that person?

PERSONAL REFLECTION. Who or what has the most influence on you? Is that influence positive or negative?

The Bible calls Christians to be controlled—not by a human leader or by the dictates of a cult, but by the Spirit of God. When we are filled by the Spirit, we will live like Jesus. *Read Ephesians 5:15-21.*

1. Paul says in verse 16, "the days are evil." Do you agree with his evaluation? Why or why not?

2. How can the command regarding wine in verse 18 be applied to other practices or areas of life?

3. How does the analogy of being "drunk with wine" (or, "under the influence of alcohol") help you understand what it means to be "filled with the Spirit"?

4. What is the difference between being controlled by a human spiritual leader and being controlled by the Holy Spirit?

5. How will a person who is filled with the Spirit act?

6. According to these verses, what is required of a person in order to be filled with the Spirit?

7. What will characterize your relationship with the Lord when you are filled with the Spirit (vv. 19-20)?

8. Verse 21 tells us that we should submit to one another. How does this command relate to the verses that precede it?

9. Describe someone you know or have read about (in the Bible or elsewhere) whom you would consider to be filled with the Spirit.

10. How can you tell whether you are filled with the Spirit?

Invite the Holy Spirit to fill you.

Now or Later

As you think back over this series of studies, what aspect of the Holy Spirit's ministry has been most challenging to you personally? Which has been most encouraging? Sometime in the next week, pray again the prayers suggested at the end of each study. Keep in step with the Spirit.

Leader's Notes

MY GRACE IS SUFFICIENT FOR YOU. (2 COR 12:9)

Leading a Bible discussion can be an enjoyable and rewarding experience. But it can also be *scary*—especially if you've never done it before. If this is your feeling, you're in good company. When God asked Moses to lead the Israelites out of Egypt, he replied, "O Lord, please send someone else to do it"! (Ex 4:13). It was the same with Solomon, Jeremiah and Timothy, but God helped these people in spite of their weaknesses, and he will help you as well.

You don't need to be an expert on the Bible or a trained teacher to lead a Bible discussion. The idea behind these inductive studies is that the leader guides group members to discover for themselves what the Bible has to say. This method of learning will allow group members to remember much more of what is said than a lecture would.

These studies are designed to be led easily. As a matter of fact, the flow of questions through the passage from observation to interpretation to application is so natural that you may feel that the studies lead themselves. This study guide is also flexible. You can use it with a variety of groups— student, professional, neighborhood or church groups. Each study takes forty-five to sixty minutes in a group setting.

There are some important facts to know about group dynamics and encouraging discussion. The suggestions listed below should enable you to effectively and enjoyably fulfill your role as leader.

Preparing for the Study

1. Ask God to help you understand and apply the passage in your own life. Unless this happens, you will not be prepared to lead others. Pray too for the various members of the group. Ask God to open your hearts to the message of his Word and motivate you to action.

2. Read the introduction to the entire guide to get an overview of the entire book and the issues which will be explored.

3. As you begin each study, read and reread the assigned Bible passage to familiarize yourself with it.

4. This study guide is based on the New International Version of the Bible. It will help you and the group if you use this translation as the basis for your study and discussion.

5. Carefully work through each question in the study. Spend time in meditation and reflection as you consider how to respond.

6. Write your thoughts and responses in the space provided in the study guide. This will help you to express your understanding of the passage clearly.

7. It might help to have a Bible dictionary handy. Use it to look up any unfamiliar words, names or places. (For additional help on how to study a passage, see chapter five of *How to Lead a LifeGuide Bible Study*, InterVarsity Press.)

8. Consider how you can apply the Scripture to your life. Remember that the group will follow your lead in responding to the studies. They will not go any deeper than you do.

9. Once you have finished your own study of the passage, familiarize yourself with the leader's notes for the study you are leading. These are designed to help you in several ways. First, they tell you the purpose the study guide author had in mind when writing the study. Take time to think through how the study questions work together to accomplish that purpose. Second, the notes provide you with additional background information or suggestions on group dynamics for various questions. This information can be useful when people have difficulty understanding or answering a question. Third, the leader's notes can alert you to potential problems you may encounter during the study.

10. If you wish to remind yourself of anything mentioned in the leader's notes, make a note to yourself below that question in the study.

Leading the Study

1. Begin the study on time. Open with prayer, asking God to help the group to understand and apply the passage.

2. Be sure that everyone in your group has a study guide. Encourage the group to prepare beforehand for each discussion by reading the introduction to the guide and by working through the questions in the study.

3. At the beginning of your first time together, explain that these studies are meant to be discussions, not lectures. Encourage the members of the group to participate. However, do not put pressure on those who may be hesitant to speak during the first few sessions. You may want to suggest the following guidelines to your group.

☐ Stick to the topic being discussed.

☐ Your responses should be based on the verses which are the focus of the discussion and not on outside authorities such as commentaries or speakers.

☐ These studies focus on a particular passage of Scripture. Only rarely should you refer to other portions of the Bible. This allows for everyone to participate in in-depth study on equal ground.

☐ Anything said in the group is considered confidential and will not be discussed outside the group unless specific permission is given to do so.

☐ We will listen attentively to each other and provide time for each person present to talk.

☐ We will pray for each other.

4. Have a group member read the introduction at the beginning of the discussion.

5. Every session begins with a group discussion question. The question or activity is meant to be used before the passage is read. The question introduces the theme of the study and encourages group members to begin to open up. Encourage as many members as possible to participate, and be ready to get the discussion going with your own response.

This section is designed to reveal where our thoughts or feelings need to be transformed by Scripture. That is why it is especially important not to read the passage before the discussion question is asked. The passage will tend to color the honest reactions people would otherwise give because they are, of course, supposed to think the way the Bible does.

You may want to supplement the group discussion question with an ice-breaker to help people to get comfortable. See the community section of *Small Group Idea Book* for more ideas.

You also might want to use the personal reflection question with your group. Either allow a time of silence for people to respond individually or discuss it together.

6. Have a group member (or members if the passage is long) read aloud the passage to be studied. Then give people several minutes to read the passage again silently so that they can take it all in.

7. Question 1 will generally be an overview question designed to briefly survey the passage. Encourage the group to look at the whole passage, but try to avoid getting sidetracked by questions or issues that will be addressed later in the study.

8. As you ask the questions, keep in mind that they are designed to be used just as they are written. You may simply read them aloud. Or you may prefer to express them in your own words.

There may be times when it is appropriate to deviate from the study guide.

For example, a question may have already been answered. If so, move on to the next question. Or someone may raise an important question not covered in the guide. Take time to discuss it, but try to keep the group from going off on tangents.

9. Avoid answering your own questions. If necessary, repeat or rephrase them until they are clearly understood. Or point out something you read in the leader's notes to clarify the context or meaning. An eager group quickly becomes passive and silent if they think the leader will do most of the talking.

10. Don't be afraid of silence. People may need time to think about the question before formulating their answers.

11. Don't be content with just one answer. Ask, "What do the rest of you think?" or "Anything else?" until several people have given answers to the question.

12. Acknowledge all contributions. Try to be affirming whenever possible. Never reject an answer. If it is clearly off-base, ask, "Which verse led you to that conclusion?" or again, "What do the rest of you think?"

13. Don't expect every answer to be addressed to you, even though this will probably happen at first. As group members become more at ease, they will begin to truly interact with each other. This is one sign of healthy discussion.

14. Don't be afraid of controversy. It can be very stimulating. If you don't resolve an issue completely, don't be frustrated. Move on and keep it in mind for later. A subsequent study may solve the problem.

15. Periodically summarize what the group has said about the passage. This helps to draw together the various ideas mentioned and gives continuity to the study. But don't preach.

16. At the end of the Bible discussion you may want to allow group members a time of quiet to work on an idea under "Now or Later." Then discuss what you experienced. Or you may want to encourage group members to work on these ideas between meetings. Give an opportunity during the session for people to talk about what they are learning.

17. Conclude your time together with conversational prayer, adapting the prayer suggestion at the end of the study to your group. Ask for God's help in following through on the commitments you've made.

18. End on time.

Many more suggestions and helps are found in *How to Lead a LifeGuide Bible Study,* which is part of the LifeGuide Bible Study series.

Components of Small Groups
A healthy small group should do more than study the Bible. There are four

components to consider as you structure your time together.

Nurture. Small groups help us to grow in our knowledge and love of God. Bible study is the key to making this happen and is the foundation of your small group.

Community. Small groups are a great place to develop deep friendships with other Christians. Allow time for informal interaction before and after each study. Plan activities and games that will help you get to know each other. Spend time having fun together—going on a picnic or cooking dinner together.

Worship and prayer. Your study will be enhanced by spending time praising God together in prayer or song. Pray for each other's needs—and keep track of how God is answering prayer in your group. Ask God to help you to apply what you are learning in your study.

Outreach. Reaching out to others can be a practical way of applying what you are learning, and it will keep your group from becoming self-focused. Host a series of evangelistic discussions for your friends or neighbors. Clean up the yard of an elderly friend. Serve at a soup kitchen together, or spend a day working on a Habitat house.

Many more suggestions and helps in each of these areas are found in *Small Group Idea Book.* Information on building a small group can be found in *Small Group Leaders' Handbook* and *The Big Book on Small Groups* (both from Inter-Varsity Press). Reading through one of these books would be worth your time.

General Introduction to the Holy Spirit

The Bible's teaching on the Holy Spirit is extensive. As the group leader, you will find it helpful to read a survey of teaching on the Spirit. Be sure to choose material that will lead you into a deeper understanding of the biblical teaching on the subject, not just through the controversies of modern theologians. Any standard book on systematic theology will include a section on the Holy Spirit. Single volumes abound too. Three of the best are:

Robert Gromacki, *The Holy Spirit* (Nashville: Word, 1999).

Charles Swindoll, *Flying Close to the Flame: A Passion for the Holy Spirit* (Dallas: Word, 1993).

Gordon Fee, *Paul, the Spirit and the People of God* (Peabody, Mass.: Hendrickson, 1996).

Once you have a broader view of the biblical teaching on the Holy Spirit, you will be better equipped to answer questions that may arise during group discussion.

The doctrine of the Holy Spirit is also one of the most controversial areas of Christian theology. Be prepared for some disagreements in your group! It is valuable, of course, to explore all sides of a controversial issue, but strive to come back to a biblical foundation for any conclusions.

The emphasis throughout these studies should be on the student's personal response to the truth that is discovered. A question that should be asked often as you conclude a study is: "How will you live (think, act) differently as a result of what we have learned?"

Study 1. Meet the Holy Spirit! John 16:5-15.

Purpose: To introduce the student to the Holy Spirit and to the Spirit's ministry.

Question 1. The leader should read through chapters 13—17 in John's Gospel as part of the preparation for this study. Jesus spoke about the Holy Spirit in several sections of this discourse. Look for insights into the mood of the disciples and how Jesus' words addressed their fears and concerns.

Question 2. The Greek word translated "Counselor" is *parakletos* (para-klay-toss). You will sometimes hear the Spirit referred to as the "Paraclete." The word refers to someone who is called alongside to give assistance. It is a difficult word to translate into one English word. Other versions use the words "Comforter," "Helper," "Advocate" or "Friend."

Question 3. Jesus' personal presence was limited to those immediately around him. The Spirit, on the other hand, would be accessible to every believer. If Jesus were still on earth today, we would have to stand in line to meet with God. Since the Holy Spirit indwells each believer, we can have immediate access to God.

Question 4. The Spirit is at work whenever the message of Christ is proclaimed to convict or to convince those who hear of the truth of the message. The Spirit convinces those who hear that they have committed personal sin, that Jesus is the only righteous one, and that judgment will come upon those who refuse Christ's offer of salvation.

Question 5. Satan's condemnation was made certain by Jesus' death and resurrection. He is still around and very active but he is a defeated enemy. Those who refuse to follow Jesus have linked their lives and destinies to a condemned leader.

Question 7. Jesus makes it clear that the Spirit would have a special ministry to his closest followers to remind them of Jesus' teaching and to lead them into the truth. Jesus placed his stamp of approval on the words of the apostles before those words were ever written down as our New Testament Scriptures.

Question 8. Jesus speaks of the Counselor as an equal to himself and the Father. This is indirect testimony to the Spirit's deity. Jesus also speaks of the

Spirit as a distinct person rather than simply a force or the expression of God's power. Another significant point to emphasize is that the Spirit's function is to exalt and glorify Jesus. The Spirit is present when Jesus is lifted up.

Study 2. The Spirit Invades. Acts 2.

Purpose: To help us understand the Spirit's powerful coming on the day of Pentecost and to show how that event affects our lives today.

Group discussion. Personal experiences of the Spirit's moving will vary widely. Some may have seen outward evidences of the Spirit's work as people were moved to repentance or faith in Christ. Some may have seen miraculous events. Others may have been quietly moved to renewed commitment to Christ or to a new level of devotion. Allow individuals to share briefly in order to get the group thinking about the Spirit's sweeping power.

Some in the group may question the Spirit's presence and activity in the world *before* this event in Acts 2. Remind them of the Spirit's activity in creation (Gen 1:2), his empowering work in the Old Testament (Judg 15:14), his work of guiding God's people (Is 63:10), and the Spirit's ministry to Jesus (Mt 4:1). We say the Holy Spirit "came" on the day of Pentecost, but we mean that he came upon believers in a way he had not energized them before.

Question 2. The Feast of Pentecost is a Jewish holy day instituted in the Law of Moses. It takes place fifty days after the Feast of Passover. Pentecost is also called the Feast of Weeks (see Lev 23:15-21). The feast celebrates God's provision of a new harvest. In the days of Jesus it was also viewed as the anniversary of the giving of the Law to Moses on Mount Sinai. Jews from throughout the Roman Empire came to Jerusalem for this observance.

Question 3. Christians have differing opinions on speaking in tongues. In this passage it seems clear that the early believers spoke the praises of God in the native languages of the listeners (v. 8). The variety of languages certainly pictured the universal sweep of the gospel message.

Question 4. The coming of the Spirit in a new way was not a surprise in God's plan. Just as the arrival of the Messiah had been predicted by the prophets, so s great outpouring of the Spirit had been declared centuries before it happened. The people of Israel should not have been surprised by what was happening. They should have been expecting the fulfillment of God's promise.

Question 5. The events in Acts 2 took place just seven weeks after Jesus' death and resurrection and just ten days after Jesus' ascension into heaven (see Acts 1:3). The new message of the gospel centered on the resurrection of Jesus and his exaltation to the position of Lord. Jesus' resurrection was proof that he was the Messiah from God, God's promised Deliverer.

Question 6. This verse (Acts 2:38) may create discussion (and disagreement) about the relationship between water baptism and salvation. You may want to allow some expression of each position, but that issue is not the focus of this study. The questions in the study guide focus on the results of faith in Christ, not on the process involved. The people who believed that day were baptized as evidence of their repentance and faith.

Question 7. Don't neglect to point out the attitudes of these early Christians —awe before God, praise, genuine concern for each other.

Question 8. As individuals explain what elements are missing in their church or small group, do not allow the discussion to become a gripe session. You are looking for honest evaluation but also some personal involvement and responsibility to provide a solution.

Study 3. The Spirit Speaks. 1 Corinthians 2.

Purpose: To reveal the authority of the Spirit and to show how the Spirit speaks through Scripture.

Question 2. The Roman world was filled with philosophers and religious leaders who tried to capture the allegiance of people with powerful and per-suasive arguments. In Corinth (and in nearby Athens) an appeal to human reason worked with particular effectiveness. Paul's message of a crucified Sav-ior appeared moronic when compared to these sophisticated philosophies. Paul himself appeared weak and ineffective as a speaker. The difference was that the gospel did its work! Men and women were made new as the Spirit of God drew them to faith in Christ.

Christians today can be confident of the gospel message when (1) it is accurately based on the apostles' teaching, (2) it produces a transformed life in the person who believes, and (3) the Spirit bears witness within us that we are truly children of God.

Question 3. The "wisdom of this age" refers to purely human wisdom unaided by God's truth or God's Spirit. Wisdom that ignores God leads to emptiness and irrational behavior. Wisdom from God leads to maturity and glory. Paul is not advocating an anti-intellectual attitude toward education or human wisdom. He is simply making the point that human wisdom *alone* is inadequate to answer life's deepest questions.

Question 4. Human observation and reason alone are not the right tools to use for discovering truth about God. The truth that unaided human reason has failed to discover has been revealed to us by the Spirit (v. 10).

Question 5. Just as a human being is the only person who can know himself or herself fully and completely, only God can fully know the mind and heart of God. Since the Spirit knows God thoroughly, he must himself be God.

Question 6. This passage is a key text supporting the authority and truthfulness of the apostles' writings in the New Testament. The apostles did not write their own opinions but the Spirit's words.

Question 7. A person who does not possess the Holy Spirit is incapable of fully understanding God's truth. The truth of the gospel seems foolish to those whose hearts and minds are in darkness. Only the Spirit can bring light and understanding.

Question 8. The Word of God and the Spirit of God combine to give us a great gift—the mind of Christ.

Question 10. Be sure to emphasize the importance of seeking the Spirit's enlightenment even as we study Scripture passages about the Spirit! If the Spirit was the source of the Scriptures, and if God's truth can be fully understood only with the Spirit's help, we should consciously ask the Spirit to open our minds every time we approach the Bible.

Study 4. The Spirit Renews. John 3:1-8.
Purpose: To confront the student with the necessity of the new birth from the Spirit of God.

Question 1. Nicodemus (nick-o-dee´-mus) was a member of the Jewish religious party called the Pharisees. He was meticulous in his observance of the Old Testament law. He was also a member of the Sanhedrin (the Jewish ruling council) and was, therefore, held in the highest regard by the religious leadership.

Question 2. Nicodemus had a very positive view of Jesus. He called Jesus "Rabbi"—a sign of respect. He acknowledged the reality of Jesus' miracles and the fact that Jesus was sent from God. What Nicodemus had failed to realize was that Jesus was more than a prophet or teacher. Jesus went to the heart of Nicodemus's problem when he challenged him to be born from above.

Question 3. Nicodemus could only imagine a second physical birth. He had not grasped the possibility (or necessity) of a spiritual rebirth.

Question 4. Nicodemus had placed high value on his birth in the flesh. He was a descendant of Abraham, part of God's people of Israel. Jesus makes it clear, however, that Nicodemus's first birth was not enough to bring him into God's kingdom.

Some Christians believe that when Jesus says we must be born "of water and the Spirit," he is referring to water baptism. It seems best, however, to view Jesus' reference to water in relation to our first birth. "Water" (in our mother's womb) was the necessary accompaniment to the first birth of the flesh. The "Spirit" is the necessary accompaniment to our second birth.

Question 6. The blowing wind is a powerful symbol of the active Spirit. The wind is unseen but effective. The wind is "sovereign" (that is, not under human control). The wind is seen only in its effect on those it touches. In the same way, the Spirit's work is seen in the transformed life of a believer.

Question 7. Our responsibility as Christians is to tell the message of salvation in Jesus to those around us. The Spirit is the one, however, who draws those who hear to faith in Christ. Men and women are born of the Spirit.

Question 8. Use this question as an opportunity to present the gospel if you have those in your group who have not believed in Christ. Ask someone you know to be a Christian to share the story of their salvation.

Question 9. The new birth produces new life, and life gives evidence of its presence. New life in Christ produces new desires, new habits and new behavior. Be careful to avoid legalistic answers to this question such as "Christians show they are born again by going to church every Sunday" or "Christians don't do. . ." Focus more on the believer's desire to be like Christ in every area of life.

Study 5. The Spirit Empowers. Acts 6:1-15; 7:54-60.

Purpose: To awaken in us to a new awareness of the Spirit's power and his willingness to empower us to do the will of God.

Question 2. The Spirit alone decides when he will work in power. Jesus said in John 3, "The wind blows wherever it pleases." But the Spirit will also seek a prepared person through whom to work. Stephen prepared himself by humble service in the church, by diligent study of God's Word (revealed in his speech in chapter 7), and by cultivating a life of faith and obedience toward God.

Question 3. This synagogue in Jerusalem was made up of Jews who had immigrated from Cyrene and Alexandria in northern Africa and from Cilicia in Asia Minor. Immigrant groups often formed their own meeting places for friendship and solidarity in a new land. They argued with Stephen over whether Jesus was the Messiah and what effect Jesus' death and resurrection had on the old system of worship that was centered on the Temple and the Law of Moses.

Question 4. The Spirit's help is made evident by the inability of the Jews to confuse Stephen or to make him back away from the truth. His opponents, in fact, were forced to back down from the debate.

Question 6. The Sanhedrin was the same Jewish council that a few weeks earlier had condemned Jesus (Mk 14:55) and later had tried to silence Peter and John (Acts 4:5-7, 18-20). The false accusation brought against Stephen was that he had predicted the temple's destruction and the abolition of Jewish customs. Compare Matthew 26:59-66.

Question 8. Perhaps the "easy" answer to this question is to say we would choose to be Stephen, but remind those in your group who give that answer that they will die as a result of that choice. Even if no one chooses the second answer, explore the consequences that came upon those who stoned Stephen.

Study 6. The Spirit Guides. Acts 16:1-15.

Purpose: To help us rely more on the Holy Spirit as we seek to know and follow God's will for our lives.

General Note. Christians often struggle with this issue of knowing the will of God. Much of the problem comes because we tend to view God's will as a tiny spot ("the center of God's will") or as a tightrope from which we can easily fall. It has helped me to see God's will as a path. Sometimes the path is wide. Several options may all be included in God's will. At other times the path is quite narrow as God leads us in a very specific direction. The key issues are to seek to please God in the decisions we make and to obey his Word. As we do that, we can also be confident of God's leading.

In this passage in Acts, the Spirit of God leads Paul and his companions down a fairly narrow path toward a precise objective—the proclamation of the gospel in Greece. It will help your group understand the context of the passage if you use a map to show them Paul's route through Asia Minor and into Macedonia. Any Bible dictionary or handbook will have a map of this section of Paul's second evangelistic journey. A large map or small handout map will keep everyone together as you work through the various stages of Paul's trip.

Question 1. It is important to note here that negative direction from the Holy Spirit does not indicate God's disapproval or chastening. We may be walking in obedience to God and still encounter closed doors and detours. Paul was fulfilling God's call to preach the gospel and Christians were being strengthened by his ministry, but God still closed some doors in order to point Paul toward a greater opportunity.

Question 2. This is largely a speculation question since the Bible does not tell us how the Spirit communicated, but it will give members of your group the opportunity to express their opinions on how God told Paul not to enter these regions. Were they stopped at the border and not allowed to proceed? Did the Holy Spirit speak in an audible voice? Did the whole ministry team sense the Spirit's restraint or did it come only through one member?

Question 3. Sometimes we receive direction from God as we move in a particular direction. We are either affirmed in that decision or God makes it clear that we are to change course.

Question 4. Paul now understood the purpose for the closed doors earlier.

Those regions were not ready for the message of the gospel, but people in the cities of Greece were anxious to hear. Paul on his own would probably not have traveled to Greece on this particular journey. God, however, had other plans.

Question 7. The Lord's direction to Paul was confirmed by the opening of people's hearts to the gospel. But what if no one in Macedonia had believed his message? Could he have concluded that God had not called him there?

You may need to caution the members of your group about always looking for some external confirmation of God's leading. Sometimes God may lead us into difficult circumstances. At those times all we may have is the internal confirmation of the Spirit.

Question 8. Certainly when we seek God's guidance we should pray and ask God for wisdom—and then believe that he has given wisdom to us. We should also seek in whatever decision we make to please and honor Christ. Another step might be to start moving in a certain direction to see if God opens or closes the door.

Study 7. The Spirit Liberates. Romans 8:1-27.

Purpose: To prepare us to understand and to act on our liberation in Christ from the domination of sin and our old nature.

Question 2. The law of God was not evil. It was holy and good (see Rom 7:7, 12). The problem was in our sinful nature. Whoever tried to keep God's law failed. God sent his own Son to remove the burden of the law from us by offering himself as an eternal sacrifice for our sin.

Question 3. In verses 4-9 Paul contrasts the person who has never believed in Christ ("those who live according to the sinful nature") with the person who has believed ("those who live in accordance with the Spirit"). The drag of the sinful nature on our minds and behavior is counteracted by the indwelling Spirit of God.

Verse 9 also settles the issue of the relationship of salvation and the indwelling of the Spirit. Any person who is in Christ by faith is also indwelt by the Spirit.

Question 4. The destruction of death is accomplished in two stages according to these verses. First, we were dead in our spirit toward God but now our spirit has been made alive. Second, the death of our body will be overcome by our future resurrection. In both stages the Spirit is actively involved.

Question 5. The old way of life still has a powerful attraction to it. Our flesh prods us to return to the old sinful ways. As we cultivate a lifestyle in the realm of the Spirit, however, we become more and more accustomed to a life of godliness.

Question 6. We no longer have to be afraid of God the Father or picture him sitting in heaven with a big club. We can come confidently to God because we are his children.

Question 9. Sometimes in distress or pain we don't even know what to ask from God. At those times the Holy Spirit prays for us at a level deeper than words can express. We may not even be aware of the Spirit's ministry at those times, but we can be assured of his promise. We can also be assured that the Spirit prays for us according to God's desire and purpose for our lives.

Study 8. The Spirit Equips. 1 Corinthians 12.
Purpose: To challenge us to discover and use our spiritual gifts.
Question 1. This study will likely be the most controversial in the series. The leaders need to be on guard for two potential problems that often surface in discussions about spiritual gifts.

The first potential problem is that someone will use the discussion as a platform to champion a certain position on spiritual gifts. This seems to arise most often in regard to the "sign" gifts such as speaking in tongues, miraculous healing and so on. If differing viewpoints are represented in your group, give each position the opportunity to speak but do not allow one person (or position) to dominate. The issue of spiritual gifts is much broader than simply whether or not the miraculous gifts are functioning today.

The second potential problem arises when a person uses ridicule to attack a position with which they disagree. Any discussion of spiritual truth should be marked by kindness and respect. Otherwise the very Person we are discussing, the Holy Spirit, is grieved and his power is quenched.

The Holy Spirit distributes spiritual gifts to every believer. No one is left out. But the gifts were given for the building up the body of Christ. No one is gifted for himself or herself alone. The leader should emphasize the purpose of the gifts throughout the discussion. Gifts are to be used in a practical, purposeful way to encourage other believers.

Question 3. For a detailed explanation of each of these gifts, you may want to consult Leslie Flynn, *Nineteen Gifts of the Spirit* (Wheaton, Ill.: Victor Books, 1994), or Don and Katie Fortune, *Discover Your God-Given Gifts* (Wheaton, Ill.: Chosen, 1987). Those desiring an in-depth study may want to use another LifeGuide® Bible Study, *Spiritual Gifts*.

Question 4. The proper use of spiritual gifts should contribute to the harmonious functioning of the body. Far too often, however, the issue of spiritual gifts brings division and bitter dispute.

Question 5. This question will produce several opinions. Spiritual gifts are given by the Spirit, but the Spirit can also enhance natural ability (for example, vocal talent) to produce spiritual results.

Question 7. Spiritual gifts or their results are never to be used as a measure of comparison between believers. We are gifted by God and used in ministry as he desires. The size of our ministry is irrelevant.

Question 9. Some in your group may not be able to answer this question. They can be helped to discover their gifts in two ways. First, they can work through some resource material on spiritual gifts that will help them evaluate their lives and possible gifts. Some of the tools available are listed above under the note for question 3.

Another way to discover our spiritual gifts is to become involved in various ministries as God gives us the opportunity. It is often in the process of ministry that we discover what our gifts are. The evaluation of others in the body of Christ will also help us see areas where we are most effective in ministry. You may want to take the time to go around the group and affirm the strengths and gifts you see in each other.

Question 10. Spiritual gifts are not given to hide or to hoard. God intends us to use the gifts to honor him and to build up other Christians.

Study 9. The Spirit Transforms. Galatians 5:13-26.
Purpose: To give us practical help in cultivating the fruit of the Spirit in our lives.

Question 1. Our liberty in Christ is never to be used as a cloak for sinful or selfish behavior. Our liberty is limited by our obedience to Christ as Lord and by the needs of our brothers and sisters in Christ.

Question 3. Do not allow the discussion on this question to go too far. The emphasis of the study is on the dramatic difference in character and behavior between those controlled by the sinful nature and those controlled by the Spirit of God.

Question 4. Paul does not mean that Christians are incapable of these acts or that we cease to be Christians if we commit a sinful act. His point is that people who live a life marked by these things give evidence by that very lifestyle that they are not members of God's kingdom.

Question 5. If you walk into an orchard, you can quickly discover what kind of trees are there by looking at the fruit that they produce. You discover the true nature of a person by observing the "fruit" produced in his or her life. A person who claims to be in Christ and indwelt by the Spirit will produce evidence of that claim by displaying godly character.

Question 6. Paul deliberately uses the singular ("fruit" rather than "fruits") to emphasize that every aspect of the Spirit's character should be evident in our lives. Some aspects are more evident than others, but all of them should be present to some degree.

Those who want to pursue an in-depth study of this area should see Hazel Offner's study guide *The Fruit of the Spirit* in the LifeGuide® Bible Study series.

Question 7. The sinful nature was crucified in the sense that we no longer have to live under its domination or control. We as Christians can choose to be obedient to the Spirit or to submit again to the old master's authority. When we submit to the flesh, we sin; when we submit to the Spirit, we grow in godliness.

Study 10. The Spirit Influences. Ephesians 5:15-21.
Purpose: To bring our lives into joyful submission to the Spirit of God.
Introduction. Some in your group may object to the idea of being "controlled" by the Holy Spirit. The fact is (as we have seen in studies 7 and 9), everyone is controlled by something! Those who think they are in control of their own lives are in reality controlled by their sinful nature. It is only when we submit to the Spirit's influence that we experience genuine self-control (see Gal 5:22-23).

Question 2. The point of this question is not to generate a lengthy discussion on a Christian's use (or nonuse) of alcohol! Paul's concern is the misuse of anything that takes away our ability to submit to the Spirit of God. "Addiction" in any garb is not within the realm of God's will for any Christian.

Question 3. The phrase "to be filled" was often used in the New Testament to refer to control. (See, for example, Jn 16:6 and Acts 5:3, 17.) We are not to drink so much that we are under alcohol's influence, but we are to be filled (controlled, influenced) by the Spirit.

Question 5. A Spirit-controlled person will display the fruit of the Spirit in every situation (see Gal 5:22-23). Another way to explain it is to say that in Jesus we see a perfectly Spirit-filled person. So, when we are Spirit-filled, we will act like Jesus would act if he faced the situations, people and problems we face.

Question 6. Several requirements for the filling of the Spirit can be gleaned from these verses. The person who desires to be filled with the Spirit should be walking in wisdom (v. 15) and obedience to the Lord (v. 17). Since Paul commands us to be filled with the Spirit, it is obviously a matter of choice and responsibility on our part to submit willingly to the Spirit's direction and control in our lives.

Question 8. The Spirit's control will be evident not only in our spiritual life but also in our relationships to others. Paul goes on to spell out what a Spirit-controlled marriage and home look like (Eph 5:22—6:4) and how Spirit-controlled people operate in the workplace (Eph 6:5-9).

Question 10. The filling of the Spirit is a matter of obedience, not necessarily a matter of emotion. We may not "feel" the Spirit's filling, but if we are walking in obedience to God's Word and are yielding ourselves to the Spirit, we can be confident that we are filled with the Spirit.

Douglas Connelly is a Christian writer and speaker who lives with his wife, Karen, near Flint, Michigan. He is also the author of the LifeGuide® Bible Studies Angels, Daniel, Encountering Jesus, John, Heaven, Miracles *and the books* Angels Around Us *and* The Promise of Heaven (InterVarsity Press) *and* The Bible for Blockheads (Zondervan).

ALSO FOR SMALL GROUPS

As well as over 70 titles in the popular *LifeBuilder* series, Scripture Union produces a wide variety of resources for small groups. Among them are:

WordLive – an innovative online Bible experience for groups and individuals, offering a wide variety of free material: study notes, maps, illustrations, images, poems, meditations, downloadable podcasts, prayer activities. Log on and check it out: www.wordlive.org

The Multi-Sensory series – popular resources for creative small groups, youth groups and churches that appeal to a wide range of learning styles.

Deeper Encounter – for confident groups that have a good understanding of Bible text – containing seven studies, complete with CD audio tracks and photocopiable worksheets.

Top Tips on Leading Small Groups – biblical patterns and practical ideas to inspire leaders of small groups.

Essential 100 and *Essential Jesus* – 100-reading overview of the Bible (*Essential 100*) and the person and work of Jesus (*Essential Jesus*), with notes and helps – presented as a programme for individuals, small groups or whole churches.

Small Groups Growing Churches – a flexible training resource for leading small groups. Can be used as a complete 15-topic training course, for a tailor-made church weekend or for one-off refresher sessions.

SU publications are available from Christian bookshops, on the Internet, or via mail order. Advice on what would suit your group best is always available. You can:

- log on to www.scriptureunion.org.uk
- phone SU's mail order line: 01908 856006
- email info@scriptureunion.org.uk
- fax 01908 856020
- write to SU Mail Order, PO Box 5148, Milton Keynes MLO, MK2 2YX

Scripture Union
Using the Bible to inspire children, young people and adults to know God.